MW01538332

Successful Sales
Without
Selling Your Soul

by

George W Childs

Successful Sales Without Selling Your Soul

by George W Childs

Published by Heart Gate Enterprises, LLC

© Copyright 2010, George W Childs

All rights reserved under U.S. Copyright law as well as International and Pan-American copyright conventions. No part of this publication may be reproduced, duplicated, transmitted, recorded, photocopied, scanned or stored in any way, including but not limited to current and future technological advances, without the prior written permission of the publisher (Heart Gate Enterprises, LLC). Reviewers are welcome to quote brief passages provided the book title and author's name are given, along with a link to www.GeorgeWChilds.com.

Direct all inquiries to:
Heart Gate Enterprises, LLC
7417 Richland Place
Pittsburgh, Pennsylvania 15208

Contents

Introduction

Look up "The Oldest Profession" online and you'll find that it is the sale of a "personal service" in exchange for money.

Can you imagine, then, what the first successful sale was like?

No written contract.

Cash On Delivery.

Was the customer satisfied?

Who's to say?

Unfortunately, it might have cost both buyer and seller their immortal souls.

That's a pretty high price to pay for anything.

It would be nice to think that you could sell something for a living without selling your soul.

But can you?

I used to wonder why I hesitated to choose a career in sales, and why I always balked at "selling myself".

My grandfather was a natural-born salesman.

Admittedly, he had the gift of gab. My grandmother would always say, "Your grandfather could strike up a conversation with a lamp post."

And sometimes if you watched him closely, you could see the wheels of his mind rolling through a problem on the way to its solution.

My grandfather would be figuring out whom to call next, and how he would explain his ideas. He was rehearsing and thinking about what he would say, and how he would say it.

Whenever he hit upon a solution, he emphatically explained it to others, and why he needed to make it happen ASAP. My grandfather was always passionate about his ideas, and I always loved him for his compassion. I still miss him.

One would think that having such a great role model at hand, sales would be a natural interest of mine growing up. I was interested in financial markets from the moment I learned they existed in the 4th grade, but for some reason, sales didn't appeal to me.

Perhaps my hesitation was due to the negativity that surrounds "selling" in our culture.

I used to casually tell people that I "sold out" of my retail business. However, I realized that it sounded negative. In football, you hear commentators say that the defense "sold out" on the blitz, leaving themselves exposed to a big play.

The only positivity related to selling that comes to my mind is having a "sell out" crowd, and even then the subject of ticket "scalpers" is usually close behind.

I don't remember the first time I saw a cultural reference to *Death of a Salesman*, the play by Arthur Miller. It wasn't until writing this book that I comprehended how the mere title of this play had had an impact (however subconscious) on how I thought about sales.

When I finally read the play, it felt like anti-capitalist propaganda, although Miller suggested that he wanted to explore the suicide of his traveling salesman uncle, and his relationship with his sons.

When I was younger and hadn't seen or even read the play, all I had was a title and a lot of questions:

Did all salesmen die? Well, we all do, but… And how do they die? It didn't sound good. Did he kill himself? If I go into sales, am I going to die?

Add to these visceral questions and impressions the results from surveys that show used car salesmen are second only to politicians for the contempt in which the public holds them.

The public image of the slick salesman is not a pretty one.

My grandfather, a consummate salesman, always recommended being salaried in sales. Most of us assume that if a salesman is too "hungry", he or she isn't going to care what you buy as long as you buy something.

In addition, most people don't like being pressured and some sales people come on too strong.

Once, when my wife and I were an unqualified lead for home window replacement, we were subjected to a salesman who just would not give up. It was such a horrible experience that it took us *years* to replace our windows. And we didn't use his company either.

So if you're in sales, or think you might like to be, how do you overcome this negative image?

What can you do to separate your soul from the fear that a successful sale means that you have to lie about your product? How can you succeed in sales, while remaining true to principles that you can live with?

Well, you've bought the right book.

I structured this book to maximize your effectiveness, while minimizing your reading time.

Each chapter of the first part of the book has strategies for increasing your sales that are matched up with specific tactics to help you put those strategies into practice quickly. The ideas are presented right up front, so that if you understand them right away, you can implement them immediately.

If you need a broader explanation and a more subtle understanding of the meaning, the rest of the chapter fleshes out the idea in clear and concise language. I also include stories as illustrations of the principles I use to sell successfully.

In the second part, I discuss detailed plans for living in your principles, so that you don't have to worry about your ultimate destination.

If you find your life in sales is surrounded by negativity, understand that it doesn't have to be this way.

That's why I wrote this book.

So, what changed?

How did I overcome the negative image of sales as a profession, and learn to understand my grandfather after all these years?

Read on.

Part I

Strategies
&
Tactics
To Master

Chapter 1

"Always be in sales!"
- Granddaddy

My maternal grandfather, Granddaddy as we called him, is the true inspiration for this book. I got to know him pretty well over the years, and I still miss him now that he's no longer with us.

He was a business insurance salesman who set out with a couple of savvy partners to start their own insurance brokering company after the War. Together they were true innovators who helped other businesses to manage their risks, while maintaining a level of customer service unmatched in the industry.

They paid off an angel investor within six months and never looked back.

One day, after he had retired from his long and successful career, my grandfather was talking to me about the work he was doing to raise money for a local hospital foundation. I was in high school and thinking about my career options. I'll never forget him telling me:

"Georgie, my boy, always be in sales!"

"What do you mean, Granddaddy?"

"Look, you know I retired a few years ago."

"Yes."

"Well, I never stopped working. Take the hospital foundation I'm directing, for instance. I'm busier than ever trying to raise money to provide education, new equipment, and better communications so that the patient care is constantly improving. Even though I retired from sales, I'm still in sales."

It took a few years and a good deal more experience for the real lesson to sink in for me. The principles involved in successful sales were the same ones that made it easier for me to communicate with and understand people in my everyday life.

When I wrote an essay in school, I was in sales. Every day that I made a graph to explain a concept at work, I was in sales. Whenever I put together a resume or went on a job interview, I was in sales. Each time I taught a class or gave a presentation, I was in sales.

Being in sales means interacting with people and communicating ideas. Everyone is in sales every day…but they don't always recognize it.

Now that you know you're in sales (along with everyone else whether they want to recognize it or not), what's the one thing you can do to improve your sales every day?

Practice what you pitch.

You need a go-to sales pitch that you know inside and out, backwards and forwards. You need a pitch that you can deliver to anyone whether you're in an elevator or jogging down the street.

There are an infinite number of pitches available, but you need to know *your* pitch cold. And the best way to know a pitch cold is to practice, practice, practice, and practice.

When you finish practicing, practice some more. Have I mentioned that you need to practice?

Start out by writing down your pitch. Read it out loud. Does it sound conversational? Does your pitch make sense to someone who doesn't know you well or what you do?

Next, try it out in front of a mirror. Have you memorized it so that you can watch yourself in the mirror as you deliver it? Look yourself in the eyes as you practice your pitch.

After you have written and practiced your pitch, you should add two steps that most people won't do even if they do practice (and most people don't practice).

First, time yourself to make sure that you can present your idea or offer coherently in less than a minute.

Second, take video of yourself making your pitch so that you can see yourself as others see you. It may make you nervous at first, but it will simulate how you will feel when you talk with others.

If it still makes you nervous, keep practicing. Besides, it'll come in handy at cocktail parties when people ask you what you do.

"All the world's a stage," as Shakespeare quoted the cliché years ago.

Be a player.

When I went to France to study for my junior year in college, my goal was to learn to talk and act like a native. I was afraid of being labeled as the Ugly (and Ignorant) American tourist that I had heard about in the media and from my teachers in school.

However, even after years of book learning, my French accent was outrageous and my vocabulary was worse. If I was to avoid being labeled, I needed to practice speaking French, and more importantly to practice *being* French.

During the first semester, I hung out mostly with American students as I tried to adjust to my life in France.

I realized, however, that this was no way to *be* French. So, I got to know some French students socially. I would talk with them during breaks between classes.

Soon, I was invited to parties and dinners. I went to "football matches" so that I could hang out more with my fellow French students.

I even helped a French graduate student who was researching papers written in English about the British National Health Service. I helped her to understand some of the subtler nuances of the Brits' conclusions. I improved my French social skills, and got a nice lunch out of the deal.

To really *be* French, however, what I needed to do was to practice every day the everyday language that French people used with each other.

So as I walked from bar to café or café to train station or train station to post office, I would practice the everyday language of interacting with French people: shop clerks, ticket takers, street vendors, and waiters, etc. I would play out scenarios in my mind of what I would ask for and what kind of responses I would get in return.

Sometimes I got an unexpected response, but after a while I could easily figure out a way to return to one of the scripts I had practiced over and over and over again in my imagination.

To succeed in sales, you need to practice in the same way—practice, learn, and adapt.

One weekend, I was visiting in Paris when I decided to grab a cup of hot chocolate in a café in the Latin Quarter on the left bank of the Seine River.

Students have been hanging out drinking coffee in the Latin Quarter since the French figured out how to make espresso in the 19th century.

In France, café-hopping is a national sport. You sit down by the window, or at the tables outside a café, and spend the next hour or so watching people walk by.

You can read or write, or even talk with your friends, but what you're really doing is checking out all the people walking by. They know you're checking them out. You know you're checking them out, and everyone pretends not to notice.

I took a table by the window. I was going to pretend to write as I people-watched, so I brought out my journal and my pen. Knowing exactly what I was going to order, I looked up expectantly as the waiter approached.

Warning: the following dialogue contains actual French words…the translation following each line is subject to interpretation.

"Monsieur?"

By this the waiter meant to say, "Hello sir, what can I get for you today?"

"Oui Bonjour, je voudrais un chocolat chaud, s'il vous plait."

I responded in the most polite manner possible, "Yes hello, I would like a cup of hot chocolate, please."

"Un chocolat?"

Note that I had requested a HOT (chaud) chocolate, and the waiter responded using two words with the following meaning, "You silly American, you don't need to use the word hot when ordering hot chocolate in a Parisian café. We don't serve cold chocolate here!"

"Oui, un chocolat."

Yes, a chocolate, of course it will be hot. How silly of me to think that you might sell chocolate candy bars in a café.

I quickly made a mental note.

Again, I would have to practice, *and* I had to learn and adapt.

Two weeks later I was back in Paris and decided to go to the same café to test out my adaptation. I sat down at the same table, at the same time of day, and began to pull out my journal and pen. Indeed, my favorite waiter approached casually.

"Monsieur?"

By this the waiter meant to say, "Ah, I see you have returned, sir, what can I get for you today?"

"Oui Bonjour, je voudrais un chocolat, s'il vous plait."

And this time my response meant (again politely), "Yes hello, I would like a cup of hot chocolate, please. I also learned from our last encounter that I don't have to waste time actually using the French term for HOT when I'm ordering. Thanks."

"Un chocolat…chaud?"

Once again another valuable lesson to learn in his response: "You are still a silly American, and you should know better than to try to please a Parisian waiter. We get paid for attitude."

Always practice your sales pitch. Always focus on the best way to close your sale. And remember, sometimes *you* are the customer.

So, what was my payoff for learning how to *be* French?

Well, I achieved my goal of *being* French several times during my junior year abroad (and it wasn't just about not bathing, becoming thin, eating cheese, and drinking Perrier).

With the help of a French graduate student in the language laboratory, I was finally able to hear my mispronunciations. Later, a French train conductor mistook me for a native and berated me for letting foreigners ride at peak times with a non-peak train ticket.

One of the French parents told me I didn't have an accent anymore, and a friend of mine told me that I sounded like a Frenchman from the countryside over the phone. At least I didn't sound Swiss.

I didn't understand then that I was in sales. However, I was still able to take the same approach that my grandfather took. In France, my goal was cultural, and so was my payoff.

Now that you've read and understood the first chapter, you know that you're in sales whether your job title is "agent", "principal", "customer service representative", or "student". And better still you know that to succeed, whatever you do, you need to practice what you pitch.

So, how do you get paid?

Chapter 2

Selling is service

Why would customers pay you unless you can do something for them or provide them with something?

They wouldn't.

To get paid, you need to focus on supplying the needs of your customer. If you do so, you will sell more. This is a fundamental truth.

My high school Latin teacher, Ray Sotak, put this truth another way:

"We are on this earth to serve others."

I struggled for a long time trying to understand what Mr. Sotak meant.

High school teachers are famous for trying to get hormone-addled teenagers to think about something besides sex, drugs, and rock 'n' roll. Was he trying to enlighten us in some other way?

At first, I took his statement literally. Are we all supposed to become waiters? What if I don't want to grow up to be a doctor? I can't stand seeing other people injured or sick.

I'm pretty sure my friend doesn't want to take over his parents' hair salon. What's he going to do? What does it mean to "serve others"?

My Economics teacher, on the other hand, was always lamenting that we were exporting all of our manufacturing jobs overseas to Japan. "What are we going to do in this country ten years from now," he would intone, "serve each other all day at McDonald's?"

Today, we talk about China making and exporting everything. Last decade, it was Mexico. Policy wonks have been droning on about "the decline of manufacturing" as long as I can remember.

In the 19th century, the Luddites were worried about machinery taking the jobs of tradesmen and craftsmen. Today, manufacturers use robots instead of people whenever possible, whether it's making cars or candles, tables or trinkets.

More recently I saw an article about a nursing home that purchased an automated medication dispensing system. It reduces mistakes in dispensing prescriptions to its elderly residents.

It wasn't until much later that I appreciated that my Latin teacher wasn't really contradicting my Economics teacher.

Mr. Sotak was indeed seeking to enlighten us. Like my grandfather exhorting me to always be in sales, my Latin teacher was making the point that everyone gets paid by helping people in some way.

Getting a customer to close on a deal is serving her needs.

Whether you're selling a product or a service, if you're in sales, you're providing a service both to your company and to your customers.

You generate revenue for your company by understanding what you're selling, and you're also providing a service to your customers by showing them how useful your company's product or service can be to them, as long as they sign on the dotted line.

Later, when I was in graduate school, I learned how to use math models to describe how an economy produces all the different products and services that exist.

I learned that all of the models needed a method to describe what customers were willing and able to pay in order to figure out the prices of all the products and services.

In the real world, unless buyers and sellers talk with each other about what they want, no one has any idea how much to charge for anything. Well, what customers are willing to pay for anything depends upon how much money they have, and how much they want or need any particular item.

So, if you want to sell more, you need to know what it is that your customers want and how much they're willing to pay for it. And, there is one sure-fire, time-tested, tried-and-true method to find out what your customers want.

Ask them.

Do you know what your customer wants? Ask.

When does your customer need delivery? Ask.

How much is your customer able to spend? Ask.

What else does your client need? Ask.

It doesn't get any simpler than this, and that's not to say that it's always easy. For some people, asking others how much money they have to spend is like hearing nails on a chalkboard. And some customers feel the same way when asked.

This is a fundamental money attitude problem, and one that you have to fix if you're going to succeed in sales. I suggest solutions to this problem in Part II.

Now, when you ask a question, you may not always get a straight answer, but a dodged question is an opportunity to ask another question.

So, what questions are you going to ask your customers?

I thought you'd never ask!

Assess your customer first.

What is the customer's personality type? Using a combination of body language and examination of the surroundings of a customer's office or work place or home, you can determine how much time they would like to spend getting to know you personally before you start concretely discussing what your customer's needs are.

If you are not wasting your customer's time, you can ask common, safe, ice-breaking questions.

The weather is the most common subject, and if it's Monday you can ask about how the weekend went. If it's Friday, you can ask about plans for the coming weekend.

You can then ask about how business or the economy is going.

Are there any family pictures or art work on display in the office that you can "ooh and ahh" over?

Try asking if your customer has any trips planned anywhere, and is it for business or a vacation?

The more raw facts that you know about your customers, the more likely you are to make the connections necessary for a successful sale and to provide the products and services that they need.

Is your customer originally from the area, or did he recently move or change jobs? Recent movers often have many more needs in a new area or business that you may be able to provide or refer.

Does your customer like sports? If you can get tickets to a preferred game, you might find it easier to land that account.

Once the ice is broken, you can better assess your customer's needs with more questions.

Does your customer currently experience any frustrations in business or at home for consumers? If so, you may have suggestions that could make life easier or business more profitable.

You may even sell one or more of them.

There's no end or limit to the questions you can ask a customer, only the amount of time you have to ask them.

Upon meeting one prospect, who knew only a little about my services, I started our meeting by asking him, "Do **you** have any questions?"

Because of his personality, this question launched him into a long explanation of what he was looking for. All I had to do was listen for the end of his monologue and hand him the paper to sign.

Now, clearly he was presold and ready to sign on. But if I had gotten in the way and wasted time trying to sell him on a service he already wanted to buy, he might have become annoyed and refused to sign. He didn't want to hear that much about me except to know that I understood him. He also had a strong desire to tell his story, especially to someone with a sympathetic ear.

By listening, I was able to help him talk himself into using my services.

Asking questions and then listening intently to the answers puts you in a position to serve your customer at your best.

We are indeed on this earth to serve others, at least for a time, and we can learn how to serve them best by asking them questions, and then listening attentively to their answers.

Chapter 3

Set goals, like Santa

If you are currently part of a good sales organization, then you're familiar with setting goals.

Any sales organization worth its salt sets revenue goals for each month, quarter, and year. Then it monitors performance to ensure goals are met or to change direction in case of failure.

What you may not be so familiar with, is actually achieving your revenue goals, especially in a slow economy or a declining industry.

Football analogies always spring to mind: "We need a first down this week," or "To save this quarter's sales figures, we're going to need to throw a *Hail Mary!*" What we really need are achievable goals, rather than slogans or cheerleading.

I was once asked to comment on a goal-oriented statement:

"Your reach should always exceed your grasp."

When I first considered my own "reach" and "grasp", I took it to mean that I should always be seeking to improve myself, to go beyond my comfort zone.

Having experienced both reaching and grasping over the years, I understand now that there are times to strive to improve and there are other places where it is best to rest comfortably.

Now, what does this statement mean in the context of setting goals?

Well, if you were a really lousy sales manager who wanted to drive his sales force crazy, you would always set a sales goal that was impossible for your team to reach.

It's okay to throw a *Hail Mary* pass at the end of the game when time is running out and results are critical. However, expecting miraculous results every period of every sales forecast does more harm than good. If your sales people exceed their goals, you need to reward their strong performance.

The truth about any business is that it has to make money to stay in business.

This will always require revenues that are ultimately driven by sales. No sales, no business. Every business needs achievable sales goals, and if they aren't being met, then the salespeople will be the first to go.

Of course, goals are important in more areas than just traditional sales jobs.

If you think back about how you got into sales, you may have had some goals that you set for yourself that made sales an attractive career choice.

If you have yet to set personal goals in your own life, you will find my friend Evan Frasier's *The Frasier Formula for Success* to be a useful tool for setting goals and following through on achieving them as well.

Goals are important for planning what your next steps will be and laying the groundwork or foundation for achieving them. At the same time, how do you "stay in the moment" in order to get your work done?

Well, here the key is *focus*.

We live in a world today where technology offers us the means to move 100 miles an hour in every area of daily life. We can text while driving, we can eat while watching TV or surfing the Internet, we can run while listening to music, or we can try to sleep on a redeye flight from coast to coast.

It's called multitasking and it always sounds like a bargain in our "not-enough-time-in-the-day" 24/7 world.

I love two-fers. It makes you feel like you're getting something for nothing.

Beware of multitasking, however.

You will always run the risk that you do neither of the "tasks" well and then you'll have to do one or the other over again anyway.

It is almost always better to do one task at a time and to really focus on that single task at hand. Typically, you will get it done faster, and then you'll have more time, energy, and focus for the next task at hand.

If you have more than one thing that has to be done at the same time, see if you can farm it out to an assistant or someone outside your direct employment. I discuss outsourcing in more detail in Part II.

Focus is even more critical if your task is related to succeeding in sales.

If you're talking to a prospect, make sure that you focus on listening to what he is telling you. If there's something he's not telling you, keep asking questions until he does.

Our challenge is today's highly distracting world. How can we concretely maintain our focus so as to finish a task, so that we can succeed in sales?

Well, the guy that brings you all of the toys and gadgets every year at Christmas time can also show the way when it comes to focusing. That's right, Santa Claus.

Be Santa—every day.

Now, Santa Claus, if you take a moment to consider him, has a *lot* going for him. He gets tons of free marketing. He's got more helpers in more places than any CEO in history. And Santa gets more done in one night than most people can even dream possible. How does he do it?

We know from the Christmas classic *Santa Claus Is Coming To Town* that Santa's got a list of all the boys and girls, the naughty and the nice. And after he makes his list, he checks it twice.

So, what can we learn from Santa that can give us more successful sales every day—not to mention help us better focus on the task at hand today?

Make a list and then check it twice to make sure that you get your list done.

I purchased the retail portion of a business from a successful guy who wanted to retire.

In the days before Post-it® notes, this guy had custom-printed paper pads with the company logo on them and "Get It Done Today" at the top of each page. Below that was a slot for a name and a date, 10 lines for a to-do list, and check boxes for the completion of each item on the list.

He could hand these out all day, or just make a list for himself each day to make sure he didn't miss anything. I sold the business years ago, but I still use these pads every day.

When I run out of them, I'm going to get custom-made Post-It® notes in the same style.

Checking your list twice means checking by lunchtime to see how much progress you're making, then checking by the end of the day to make sure it all got done.

Constant monitoring can make sales teams resentful and little kids paranoid at Christmas.

What you **do** need is accountability when reaching for your goals so that you can make effective changes to your actions when needed.

Checking up with accountability also makes clear what direction you need to reach toward in order to grasp the next rung on the ladder to your successful sales.

Chapter 4

FACE your stress

Okay, now you have set your goals and you have your checklists ready to go.

What happens when conflicts arise?

What do you do first when two or more different priorities demand your immediate attention?

When conflict arises, most of us try to find some way to either avoid it or another way to go around it. Ideally, we would resolve it cost-effectively.

Personally, I have always shied away from conflict. In grade school I did my best to steer clear of bullies.

I was lucky enough to play hockey as a kid, but I quit after middle school because I had seen high school players fighting on the ice.

I knew it wasn't for me.

Why do so many people shy away from confrontation and conflict?

Because it makes us feel uncomfortable.

Conflict and the stress that comes with it cause physical sensations in our bodies that involve what psychologists refer to as the "Fight or Flight" response. By avoiding conflict, we can at least temporarily return to our "normal" comfortable state.

Some conflicts, however, seem unavoidable and not of our own choosing.

How can we safely resolve them?

Not all conflicts involve violence of any kind, thankfully. The most common conflicts in business are related to time scheduling and prioritizing workflow, although personality conflicts are also common.

Rather than avoid these conflicts (hoping that they would resolve themselves), I have found it much more effective to *FACE* them.

What does this *FACE* acronym stand for?

FACE represents four steps to conflict resolution.

*F*ree your mind.
*A*djust your attitude.
*C*hange what you can.
*E*njoy your freedom.

Remembering this acronym, you will see how to resolve conflicts even as they happen.

*F*ree your mind!

Free you mind from its immediate constraints.

Some people like to call this "thinking outside the box", but I'm referring to infinite possibilities.

Begin by asking yourself questions about how the conflict arose. Was it inevitable?

Are there any immediate actions that you can take to at least temporarily resolve the conflict, preventing it from becoming a crisis? What is the worst possible result of the conflict?

If you weren't afraid of the possible outcomes, what would you do?

Allow yourself time to "sleep on it" if you can.

Free your mind and the rest will follow.

I discuss practical methods for freeing your mind in the first chapter of Part II.

*A*djust your attitude!

People always talk about bad behavior and trying to change what is observable. We have to do this in employment law. However, my experience as an employer taught me that bad behavior most often results from a bad attitude.

If you can change your attitude, you can change anything.

Your change in attitude is reflected in actions that you take. Act in alignment with your principles even if it's acting on something that seems relatively small or trivial.

Sometimes the fear surrounding a conflict can paralyze you like a deer in the headlights.

You can resolve many conflicts simply by taking a few steps in one direction or another.

*C*hange what you can!

Change what you can in your situation, and leave the rest to others.

This simple thought pattern has saved millions of people untold quantities of stress through wisdom.

Choose to be an agent of change when it is possible to do so.

Understand that the rest of the world is not your responsibility. Allow others to do what they can.

Pray for the wisdom to be able to discern what you can and cannot change.

At the same time, associate with people whom you trust in order to find a solution or to alleviate the temporary pressure. These people whom you trust may also help point the way to resolving a longer-term problem or a larger issue.

*E*njoy your freedom!

To enjoy something can mean to benefit from it. In this case, however, I implore you to put *joy* into your new freedom.

You'll have renewed energy to make choices and to take actions.

This is how my Granddaddy was able to communicate and demonstrate his solutions to his partners and customers.

As you become better at discerning and choosing which actions you can take and which ones are best left to others, focus on enjoying your choices.

So how can ***FACEing*** life's pressures and conflicts help us in a practical sense, or on a tactical level?

Let's start with the most critical decision we make every day: How do we most effectively use our time?

Time management has always fascinated me.

I remember watching an old Saturday Night Live skit where they poked fun at President Carter's attempt to convert the entire U.S. to the metric system of measurement in a few short years.

The skit lampooned that the government was distributing stimulants so that we could shift to a 100-hour day from the natural 24. "Just think how much you can get done in a Metric Day!"

Thankfully, it was just a joke.

I struggled with time choices throughout high school, trying to squeeze in all my activities between bus rides.

College was easier since I no longer had to commute. Later, when I was in graduate school, time decisions became my focus of study.

How can people solve their time conflicts?

Money can help you here.

If you have a whole bunch of it, you can skip the security hassles of commercial airlines and save time by flying in private jets like some corporate executives do.

Most people in the U.S. pay to use a time machine called an automobile, while others use public transportation or bicycles to achieve a similar effect.

However, trading money for time can work only up to a point. You can have a caddy tee up your ball and hand you a club, but to play golf you have to take the time to swing a club.

Experience has always been the best teacher and it holds office hours from moment to moment and day by day.

In sales, you need to budget your costs, and you need to budget your time. If you can identify successful salespeople in your market or industry and find out how much time they spend on their different sales activities, this can save a lot of effort and time.

For example, find out if they cold call at all, and if so, how much time they devote to it every week.

What's their average rate of successful sales for their leads? How much do they pay others for referrals? How much do they charge to refer?

Now, how do we **FACE** our time conflicts directly if we don't have a ton of money, and we know there are only 24 hours in a day?

Remember.

*F*ree your mind.
*A*djust your attitude.
*C*hange what you can.
*E*njoy your freedom.

The best way to free your mind from your time conflicts is to start with the following exercise that can show you how to let go of one thing that takes up too much time.

If you've never done a time diary over the course of a few days, go ahead and start one now.

If you feel that you don't have time to make one, you need to have started your time diary last week.

Anyway, start with today.

What did you spend your time doing today? How long did it take you to wake up? How long did it take you to get ready for work or school? How long did it take you to commute?

Once you got to work, how long did it take you to get past the water cooler, get settled, and actually start working?

How long did it take you to stare at your computer screen, play solitaire, or some other distraction before you responded to your e-mail?

Did you start making follow-up calls? Or, did you distract yourself because you dread having to do something stressful on your list of things to do?

After work, how long did it take you to get home?

Did you have useful errands to make, or were you just avoiding getting back home? (I used to be addicted to shopping at *The Home Depot*)

Did you go out drinking after work? After dinner, did you watch TV, or was the TV already on during dinner?

You might not be aware of how many decisions you made today about how to spend your time.

Can you feel these questions begin to free your mind to the possibilities of what you can do if you changed one of your current activities?

Now, if you can make a time diary like this from memory for a couple of days, and make guesses as to how long you spent at each activity, then do it.

If you can't remember accurately enough, then keep your time diary for at least 3 days.

At the end of 3 days, total up the time you spent into different categories, just like you would a budget for money.

See if you can figure out which five activities (apart from sleeping and actually working productively) you spend the most time on.

Of these five activities, is there any one of them that you don't really *need* to do, and perhaps don't really even enjoy very much?

Imagine what it would feel like if you gave up that activity, and chose to do something else with that time.

Pretend that you don't know the activity exists. Does it feel like your attitude is adjusted?

Now try going without that activity for a day, doing something else you never feel like you have the time for instead.

Can you make this one change?

I was really lucky recently when a podcast I listened to obsessively on a daily basis went from being available for free through the *iTunes* store to being limited to paid subscribers only.

It was an affordable, nominal fee, but it made me think about the time I spent listening to the podcasts and what else I could do with that time instead. As it turned out, just thinking was time better spent. Reading was also a good choice.

Ultimately, not listening to the podcast gave me more time to be present with my family.

Consider another example.

If you're paying attention to the media at all, you know that there is an obesity epidemic in America.

If Americans spent just one half hour per day exercising instead of watching TV, obesity would evaporate in less than a year.

Think about that for a moment, and then consider the implication for yourself as an individual. Imagine that, one change—swapping out one activity for a more productive one—can have a *huge* impact on your quality of life.

So for now, try making one change just for today.

Make one change.

If you keep your one change, and do it again tomorrow, try keeping it the next day.

By the end of the week, you'll be able to look back to this moment in time and feel the impact.

Enjoy the new freedom that this choice gives you every day, one day at a time.

After a month, when your change has become a habit, consider making another beneficial change.

For most people any change is initially perceived as a loss.

What you'll find is that each change you consciously choose to make brings with it a new feeling of freedom and empowerment.

Later, when you stop to smell the roses, you will appreciate how much progress you've made along the way.

Chapter 5

Listen and follow-up

Have you ever been in the middle of a sale and realized that you haven't heard what your customer just said?

Did you even know whether or not your customer asked you a question?

If you were fast on your feet, you might have figured out a clever question that got your customer to repeat himself. Well, if your mind had wandered off to begin with, your chance for a successful sale can be pretty slim.

If you don't know *why* you became distracted as you were listening to your customer, then you need to figure it out before you will succeed in sales. I discuss solutions to distraction problems in Chapter 7.

For now, we want to focus on listening.

How does listening—actively and intently—help us succeed in sales?

There are two keys to this.

First, you need to know if your customer is a qualified buyer.

Is your customer financially (and even emotionally) ready to buy? Does he have all the information he needs to make a decision? Are you talking to the decision-maker who has the budget big enough to pull the trigger?

Second, you need to find out what your customer needs and how many ways you can service those needs effectively.

Do you need to provide more customer education? Are there up-sell opportunities? Are you servicing a need that is a symptom of a much larger need that you can also service? Are there ways to involve other vendors that would provide synergy and make an even bigger sale?

I gave you some of these questions in Chapter 2. Once you ask these questions, you also need to be ready to listen and understand the answers.

In addition to making sure that you are providing what your customer really needs, your customer will understand that you're not just going to sell and run.

You will establish a relationship—one that can generate future repeat business, as well as referrals.

Okay, now that you know what your customer needs from you, how do you make sure that you are the one who makes the sale both today and in the future?

It's all about follow-up.

Consider prospects you haven't closed yet.

Are they waiting for you to get back to them with anything? Do you have a system for tracking these prospects?

If you're not using internet or computer-based software for this already, are you at least making notes in your calendar about when you should next check up on these prospects?

Do you have an assistant to help you with follow-up?

Imagine for a moment that you're one of your own customers and perform an audit of your communications system. You need to periodically test all of the links in your chain of communications from lead generation to the close of the deal.

Your weakest link might be e-mail, or it could be the automated message system that frustrates your customers. Is your receptionist getting the job done?

How hard is it to get in touch with you?

What can happen if you don't follow up with all of your communications links?

If one of your competitors is soliciting some of your busy customers and you're not following up with them, from whom are they going to buy?

When I first started running the retail business I bought years ago, I often ran around like a chicken with my head cut off. I'd put out one fire, only to find another crop up in some other part of the business.

I didn't recognize that I spent most of my time in what Stephen Covey called the "urgent and important quadrant" in his book *The 7 Habits of Highly Effective People*. That quadrant is not a place where you want to live if you want to be effective at what you do. It's a tough place to make decisions all the time, but it's a place where many people live the majority of their lives.

I know I am a frustrating customer to many of the salespeople I meet. However, the ones who make a successful sale are the ones who follow-up consistently so that they are there when I am ready to buy.

Timely follow-up is the best way of keeping the "important" issues and tasks out of the "urgent" column.

When you deal with "important" issues before they become "urgent", then there are fewer fires to put out. You can spend more time growing your sales revenue, instead of keeping it from falling.

Chapter 6

Know what you're selling, and how

You're sitting down with your prospect, enjoying a tasty lunch.

You're past the small talk because you and your prospect discovered that your kids are on the same little league team. Your prospect is definitely in the market for your company's services.

Now it's finally time to move in for the close.

Then your prospect says to you:

"Listen, I have to tell you that yesterday I received a promotional offer from your competitor, and it really sold me on trying him out. So, why should I buy from you?"

Your eyes blink momentarily, as you become aware that your prospect knows more about your market than you thought.

If you don't understand your competitors' price points and value propositions, if you don't know every product and service that you can offer, if you don't understand your company's cost structure, if you don't know your company upside down and backwards, then this will happen to you.

Well, if you can think quickly, you might be able to tap dance your way through, or your prospect might bail you out if you ask about your competitor's offer.

If you have to go do research before answering the question and that requires another meeting, what happens to the probability of a successful sale?

Will your prospect even respect you enough to return your phone calls when it's clear that you don't know everything about the company you sell for, or its competitors?

Just like when you were in school, you won't get paid for doing your homework, but doing your homework well always pays off in the end.

Now let's consider one of the most common conflicts in business as it relates to selling: timing.

Most customers will ask a sales rep, "What's your lead time; how soon can I get it?"

Overpromising and underdelivering are two sides of the same problematic coin when you're in sales.

Salespeople overpromise for fear of losing a sale, and then customers feel betrayed when the company underdelivers.

There must be enough feedback and communication between sales and production so that customers get what they paid for when they need it.

One commonly used sales strategy is to underpromise.

If sales aren't in sync with production, then this coordination gap needs to be fixed.

For example, when I had my retail business, we had a standard service delivery turnaround of two days. If a customer needed same-day service, we up-sold the service, although we still didn't charge enough for it.

When I took over the store, we routinely overpromised and underdelivered, depending upon the day of the week and the workflow. We often lost sales because customers got tired of waiting, and then were disappointed when we failed to deliver on time.

Going into a holiday, we had to cut way back on our promises of delivery so that customers could know if they would need to pay extra for the same-day service.

Invariably, we would be faced with a customer who hadn't been warned and felt that we had still overpromised in some way.

The first thing I had to change was the imbalance of our pricing structure. We were paying overtime to union employees, while discounting our services to bring in higher volume.

It was crushing our bottom line.

Yes, the employees got paid more during the busy seasons, but the hours were too long to sustain on a regular basis.

We adjusted our scheduled coverage for busier days and installed new equipment to reduce processing time, as well as errors.

The results were dramatic: we no longer had to underpromise before holidays; our customers no longer had to worry that we were overpromising on our standard service; and the bottom line improved.

Underpromising can be a reasonable short-term solution to an imbalance between your company's sales cycles and its production.

FACEing this imbalance will help you find a real long-term solution that can change whatever is holding you back.

Chapter 7

Get your head in the game

A few years ago, the company originally founded by Walt Disney, resurrected the American musical. They started out on cable and eventually succeeded on the big screen.

I think old Walt would've been proud.

In about a decade, it will be interesting to see how many high school productions of Disney's *High School Musical* are performed every year.

The opening song of the original movie is called "Get'cha Head in the Game". It's about preparing for a big game by staying focused on what's happening on the court, rather than all the cheering in the stands (especially the cheerleaders).

If your head's not in the game, you won't be able to score a sale.

Check yourself before you call on a potential customer. Is your mind clear and ready to listen to your customer?

Make sure that you can focus on that customer's needs instead of what you're having for dinner, or the less-than-perfect ending of that last conversation you had with your wife.

If you have trouble focusing, then you need to figure out why your head isn't in the game.

You can ask yourself questions to figure out what you need to get your head in the game for good, just like you can use questions to find out what your customer needs.

How does this translate into successful sales?

In any sale, for that matter in any conversation between two human beings, there is a moment where both parties to the sale take a leap of faith. They take a leap of faith because life is filled with many uncertainties—economists call them information problems.

When your head is in the game, you can focus on finding out what uncertainties are blocking a successful sale.

If I'm a retail customer, how do I know that the service or product I'm buying is up to the level of quality that I expect?

If I'm a wholesale customer, how can I make sure that my suppliers aren't ripping me off by charging too high a price?

If I'm buying a house, how do I know there aren't structural problems in the roof or the basement?

If I'm buying a business, how do I know there aren't issues concerning the honesty or integrity of the seller?

There are solutions to all of these information problems up to a point. As a sales person, it's your job to identify and eliminate as many of these uncertainties as possible.

How can you do this effectively?

As I discussed in the previous chapter, you must know your product or service. This is essential in any potential sale.

Next, you must know your customer. You can learn much about them online especially if you're selling to a business.

Always do your homework first. For retail customers, you can take some cues by manner of dress, manner of speech, body language, etc. At some point, however, you will reach the limits of what can be learned without asking questions directly.

At first, keep your questions general so that your customer has the option of free-associating and providing as much information as possible about as many different areas of interest as possible.

Next, have a list of specific questions that need to be answered in order for you to properly provide your product or service.

Finally, always solicit questions from your customer. Anticipate questions your customer might have, and practice answering these questions, the same way you practice your sales pitch.

Remember, practice makes perfect.

Chapter 8

Think more and help more

"All that we are is the result of what we have thought."

-- The Buddha

Does this mean that if I think I'm the smartest person in town, that it's true?

No.

Does it mean that if I think bad thoughts, that I'm a bad person?

No.

I use this quotation to illustrate how what you think about yourself in sales can influence what you do.

It's easier to understand my point by considering the fact that you are to other people what *they* think you are.

Or, as one of my psychiatrist friends says, "Transference is a bitch!"

Sigmund Freud, the 20th century's most famous psychiatrist, was a really smart guy who had some radical ideas about why people think and do crazy things.

Freud theorized that everyone forms relationships with each other based on their relationships with their parents or parental figures.

It can take a great deal of effort and time to get past transference and form a real relationship with someone else based on reality.

Well, you can play a similar game of transference in your own mind with yourself.

You "transfer" your feelings and thoughts about your parents (or parental figures) to yourself.

If you doubt that you have any worth then you will feel worthless. Worse still, you will transmit how worthless you feel to everyone that you communicate with.

Now, I've never been a fan of "fake it till you make it" or pretending that you are something that you're not. However, an honest assessment of what you are capable of might surprise you.

Focus on the truth of what you are, and what you can do.

It surprised me when I was finally able to take an honest look at what I thought of myself.

Just as you would ask questions of other people to learn about them, you can ask similar questions of yourself.

If you're reading this book, even if you're just skimming it, you already have a deep sense of how valuable you really are.

Think about that.

When you can be honest with yourself about your personal qualities as well as your flaws, then you are ready to become who you need to be.

Now that you understand how people perceive you, let's consider how they feel about you selling them something.

In Chapter 7, I discussed the information problems that cause uncertainty and issues that block you from a successful sale.

Well, as you are metaphorically walking your customer to that successful sale, keep in mind that some sales cycles are longer than others.

If there is a great deal of uncertainty in a larger sale, as with mergers and acquisitions or in contract procurement work, the sales cycle could involve many meetings and lots of face time. The reason for this is that both sides need assurance that the startup cost of the sale is worth the potential payoff of the sale.

Before the dance of negotiation begins, both sides want to be sure that they are not wasting their time.

Take baby steps in each of the meetings so that both sides can become more comfortable with each other. Until both sides can experience each other and ask a lot of questions, each person's transference will affect how they deal with each other and you.

In shorter sales cycles, remember to repeatedly give your prospect the opportunity to "sign on the dotted line".

If your prospect declines, ask "Why?" directly.

Whatever the uncertainty or question that's holding up your successful sale, get into the mind of your customer by asking questions.

What's preventing the customer from pulling the trigger on this sale?

Is the customer worried about current revenues?

Is there something in the product or service that the customer is uncertain about?

Is it an issue about quality or performance?

Is it about reliability of delivery?

Or, is price the sticking point?

Imagine yourself holding the hand of your customer as a friend or a close confidant.

Think of what your customer needs to know about your product or service in order to be comfortable buying it. Then imagine walking with your prospect through each part of what's necessary so that you both understand what it takes to feel comfortable with the process.

When you actually take your customer through the process, having imagined it already, your customer will be ready to sign.

Chapter 9

My brain is like a sieve

"My Brain is Like a Sieve" was the love ballad that marked keyboardist Thomas Dolby's shift from synth/pop to synth/funk music in the 1980s.

As soon as I heard the song's title, I understood that most thoughts flow through my brain like water running through a sieve.

A few thoughts and memories, however, are clingy. And if you have a thought that you don't like, and it gets stuck in your mind like a bad tune, it can make your brain hurt.

In school, we are often taught to change or improve the stickiness of our brain's sieve by memorizing certain kinds of facts.

I was trained to examine events statistically, and the most fundamental statistical tool is the histogram. A histogram is like playing the game Plinko on *The Price is Right* daytime TV game show where the balls "plink" down the pegboard into separate bins at the bottom.

My brain forms histograms into bar charts to count how many times I see an idea or a related event.

Whenever I encounter an idea, my brain checks its sieve to see if it has ever gotten stuck in my brain before. If I've seen the idea before, and it's not something that I've paid enough attention to, then I make a note that I need to spend a day or more reminding myself about the truth in the idea.

The truth of some ideas can be subtly different in newer contexts and experiences, so it never hurts to relearn the truth.

Your customer's brain will work similarly with the information you give her.

You may need to repeat something three or four times before she can see the truth of it stuck in her sieve. This was how advertising was supposed to work.

The problem with this approach was that the message was not always true.

Unlike most thoughts flitting through your mind, academic courses are designed with a focus in mind. For most classes the focus is determined by the syllabus or outline of the class.

A sale is structured in the same way.

The buyer and the seller start to talk about what they have for sale and what they need to buy. The conversation might start with a discussion about the weekend, the weather, the whiskey, or the fact that the Hartford Whalers no longer exist. However, their conversation exists because of the possibility of a successful sale.

I took a course in 19th-century French and European history when I was in France during my junior year in college.

Being in a foreign country was a great and scary time in my life and this particular course was a true eye opener in so many ways.

The history course was taught entirely in French at the local university in Nantes.

During the second semester when my French language ability had begun to take off, I was encouraged to take the supplemental *Travaux Dirigés* course that ran concurrently to the history course. Strictly translated, these "Directed Works" are the French equivalent of independent studies. These smaller groups promote interactions among students and professors.

Well, Nantes is at the southernmost edge of the Bretagne province, and Bretagne might as well be Ireland in terms of its climate. The Gulf Stream ensures that it doesn't snow in Nantes… except for the year I was there.

One day, the city was pummeled by 8 inches of snow and there was not a snowplow in sight.

The buses made valiant efforts to get through the piles of snow, but only a dozen students were able to make it to the smaller group class that day, along with the professor.

When he realized that he couldn't have a normal class period, the professor opened the floor to any questions we may have had concerning the coursework. One of the students asked a question about when snowplows were invented, and the conversation took off.

The professor held forth for over an hour—moving from one change into another (like the *Connections* series by James Burke on PBS in the 1970s). We discussed the impact of everything from Napoleon III building a canal system to the ingenious method used to lay the first transatlantic telegraph cable.

He explained the virtues of keeping hard copies of his electronic files and the differences between writing on a blank sheet of paper versus a word processor.

When the pace of questions slowed a bit, he then drew a verbal web connecting all of the seemingly unrelated topics we discussed over the course of the hour.

The common thread connecting our entire conversation was the battle for world hegemony between Great Britain and France during the latter half of the 19th century. During the course of the hour, the professor had been building up bits of information in our brains so that when the hour was over, it was easier for us to see his conclusion.

I was stunned and fascinated.

How did this happen?

How was the professor able to connect all of the questions and topics to a common theme?

Well, the professor was skilled in sales. He was clever enough to engage the class in a discussion while simultaneously educating us and selling us on a theory of history.

With enough sales skills and the right focus, you can use a discussion of the weather to point a prospect to a successful sale.

Part II

Soul-Saving Principles To Practice

Chapter 10

Choose your life and plan accordingly

Having finished Part I, you know what skills you need to practice to succeed in sales.

More importantly, you know that even if you're not in sales professionally, you're actually in sales every day because you have to communicate with people.

Now that you know how to succeed in sales, I want to turn your focus toward life choices based on your spirituality, so that you don't have to sell your soul.

Why would I call these principles soul-saving?

Well, what else would you call topics that include life choices, twelve-step programs, tithing, positive thinking, and truth?

In the same way that you found the first part of this book useful, I encourage you to keep an open mind while you read this second part. Although some of the ideas that I present here are not new, they are rarely applied in the context of successful sales.

Of course, they've never before been assembled in such an easily accessible volume.

At the end of Part I, I discussed that the mind sometimes has ideas that stick to it. Well, unless you've reached nirvana, or have plans to become a Zen Buddhist monk, you're also stuck with your mind.

Your parents and the government made you go to school so that you could fill your mind with a bunch of stuff and hopefully learn how to learn.

Now that you're an adult, your mind belongs to you.

You can decide what your mind is exposed to.

You choose what books you read, what and how much you watch TV. You choose other media like radio, surfing the web, and even emails.

Please make your choices carefully, and mindfully.

Human knowledge depreciates over time, just like equipment in a factory or the car you drive. You have to keep retooling your mind in life, just like the automobile engineers have to retool a car assembly line for each new model year.

You chose to retool your mind by reading this book.

Great choice!

Be sure that other choices you make to educate yourself are both useful and good for you.

Do you regularly watch violent TV shows or movies?

Do you listen to angry people yelling at each other on radio?

Do you read books or articles that conjure up negative images in your mind?

Are these choices really necessary for you to "enjoy" yourself? Or, are you filling up your mind with trivial thoughts in order to avoid more difficult ones?

Life events happen.

They trigger thoughts, and these thoughts do not always help us.

Our thoughts often move through our minds as an unregulated stream of consciousness. Thoughts and feelings of fear, anxiety, obsession, and guilt can paralyze us into inaction and confused thinking.

For example, have you ever had a phone call to make that you put off because you knew that it wasn't going to be good news, or you knew it would make you feel lousy? Often in sales we can fear rejection when we anticipate it.

I had a buyer once tell me before I showed him a sale that I was the last guy he wanted to talk with that week. He dreaded spending the time because he thought it was going to be boring and a waste of his time.

He made the visit anyway and found that it was a good buy.

There are many self-help books and programs that discuss negative thoughts and their effects on our behaviors.

What's great is that we have all these different tools today for effectively dealing with these thoughts. I have experienced some of these tools over the years.

Historically, the most common, traditional method for dealing with negative thoughts and emotions is silent meditation. The repetition of a mantra has become more popular as the integration of eastern and western practices continues.

Taking time to allow the mind to empty or to focus fully on one thing has proven to be a successful tactic for controlling or reducing the impact of negative thoughts on behavior. Meditation has been a useful tool for me in dealing with stress.

For some people, meditation can occur during exercise. They get into a zone, or experience a "runner's high".

I first became fully aware of the impact of negative thoughts and emotions on my life choices thanks to a course on sales training and personal effectiveness at *Partners Through People* near Pittsburgh, Pennsylvania. This is where I learned about the centrality of truth to the successful elimination of negativity.

Before meeting Sam Lucci, the CEO of *Partners Through People*, I had no idea that I could do anything about how negative my thoughts were about myself and other people.

I had learned and understood how my negativity made other people react negatively to me. What I didn't know was that I could do something about it.

It was a little bit like going through life with a headache, not knowing that someone had discovered aspirin. Sam's *Breakouts* resolved many of my life's headaches.

My brain didn't have to hurt most of the time. I could choose not to be in mental pain, or fear, or confusion. I later discovered that there were other analgesics for the mind.

After I bought his *Combat Conditioning*, Matt Furey introduced me to Dr. Maxwell Maltz's *Psycho-Cybernetics* (that was first published in 1960).

Athletes and celebrities often swear by hypnosis therapy in testimonials, although in my limited experience it was not personally effective.

Some people have used sensory deprivation, while others recommend biofeedback.

My point is that if you find yourself surrounded by negativity, choose to ask for help. If it's self-help, that's great. If it's professional help, get referrals.

I have even used binaural tones that are correlated with known brain activity. You can select your mood and dial it straight up into your brain through earphones using your *iPhone*.

Some of this technology sounds like science fiction!

Now it's reality.

Find out what works for you.

Back in the 1970s, one of the national advertising campaigns that ran during NFL football games was a series that promoted knowledge of the rules of the game. They showed controversial replays and then demanded, "**You** make the call!"

They were fun to watch, and probably explain why instant replay became popular enough to implement in live games since the 1990s.

Some events in life seem more important than others. We might even replay a particular moment in our head, just like an instant replay on TV.

If your thoughts are dominated by negative thinking, then many of these instant replays will be accompanied by negative thoughts.

They are not helping you.

Instead, replay the positive events of your life as practiced by Matt Furey in his book *The Unbeatable Man*.

If you find that some of your negative thoughts are repetitive, and cause stress or guilt, do some *Breakouts* with Sam Lucci at *Partners Through People*.

Unless we suffer from a dissociative mental illness like schizophrenia, we no longer have the excuse that we cannot control our own minds.

We have many choices to make, and at times they can feel overwhelming. However, it's up to us to get the help we need to sort through how we feel.

I encourage you to try any or all of the above solutions to help clear your brain and to achieve peace of mind. Fundamentally, what you need is to address the underlying reasons for the negative thoughts that pervade your mind.

They are blocking you from achieving the success you deserve.

This is one reason why I often encourage people to consider twelve-step programs as a long-term solution.

You can learn to resolve compulsive behaviors, and acquire skills that help you engage with people.

And learning to engage other people will increase your successful sales.

Whatever program you choose, you need to remember that just like the commercial, "You make the call!"

It's your life.

You can decide every single day.

Choose wisely.

Of course, your thoughts aren't the only area in life where you have to make choices.

Whether it's in your business or at home, you need a financial budget to help you make choices.

If you write it down on paper, or lay it out in a spreadsheet or keep it in your data cloud online, your budget can make clearer to you the decisions you make on a daily basis.

When I owned my retail business, I belonged to a cost management group.

We business owners would get together quarterly for a couple of days to go over our profit and loss statements from the previous quarter. By comparing my results with the results from similar businesses, I was able to see where my costs were higher than they should be.

If you're in sales, you need to budget the cost of your lead generation, your marketing, and your other expenses so that you can have enough take-home pay at the end of the month.

And of course, the same goes for your household.

One guy who inspires many people to use a budget today is Dave Ramsey with his *Financial Peace* programs.

By comparing what you spend in percentage terms with what successful budgeters spend, you can learn where you might be able to save money.

More importantly, you'll be able to make decisions rationally, rather than freaking out when "winging-it" fails. Dave has often cited the mistake that many part-time construction contractors make when they don't job-cost an estimate and include potential overruns plus an actual profit for themselves.

Remember, if you fail to plan, you are planning to fail.

Chapter 11

Keep it clean

Women in sales know that sex sells, as I described in my "Introduction" with the first-ever successful sale.

We also know that better-looking people sell more than not-as-good-looking people. Models are pretty or handsome because pretty sells.

When we consume an advertisement, we imagine that we will look better than we do because the models actually do look better than we do.

While I don't advocate plastic surgery, if you're in sales, you should at least make the most of what you've got.

This includes being in good physical condition and not eating too much. I mention them in the same sentence because they are correlated.

There's a popular TV show that chronicles the crazy lives of men in the advertising industry during the early 1960s. In one episode, the new head of sales loses a foot in a freak lawnmower accident. It is widely acknowledged by all the characters on the show that his career in advertising is over because he can no longer play golf. Without golf, he can no longer be in sales.

We no longer live in the early 1960s, thankfully, but people still make judgments based on personal appearance and apparent ability.

We've all heard the expression, "Cleanliness is next to Godliness." However, I've always preferred "A sound mind in a sound body."

I adopted the latter expression as a personal motto a few years back, and I adjusted it a bit.

Mens sana in corpore sano is how the original Latin saying is usually written. The English translation of "a sound mind in a sound body" doesn't quite capture the full meaning of the original saying.

You see, the Romans would not have drawn the distinction that we draw today between the mind and what we call the spirit. For the Romans the mind and spirit were part and parcel of the same entity.

In order to add it back, I like to add *per spiritum sanctum* at the end. Strictly speaking this means "through the holy spirit".

Apparently, the original *mens sana* expression was drawn from a quotation that was intended to have some irony. What's important about the overall meaning of the expression, however, is the essence of feeling comfortable in your own skin.

Regardless of what's happening around you, you can feel at peace and in balance.

To maintain this sense of peace or balance, I have found it most useful to have coordinated plans, not necessarily routines, in all three aspects of my life.

I need a plan of eating and exercising for my body.

I need a plan of learning for my mind.

And I need a plan of spiritual fellowship for my soul.

As I integrate my life, I find it useful to have different mentors for each of these plans.

However, the Latin word *sanus* is also translated as "clean" and is the root of the word "sanitary".

When I first started research work right out of college, I had been a messy desk procrastinator for as long as I could remember.

My mother was always telling me to clean up my room, or my closet, or my desk. Well, mostly my room. Mom and I used to laugh all the time about the *Trudy* comics in the newspaper each day. She often cut them out and kept them on the kitchen bulletin board.

My favorite all-time *Trudy* comic showed the young son in front of a coat rack grabbing his coat and saying, "Here it is Mom! I must have hung it up by mistake."

Anyway, at the job interview with my first real boss, my supervisor-to-be began the interview by apologizing for the fact that her desk was a mess.

And it was a mess.

Research papers were piled high on all sides.

Tables and graphs were laid out for inspection.

In these early days of PC use, no one could quite figure out how to work with a huge box on or near their desk and a clumsy keyboard at an awkward angle.

Never missing an opportunity to suck up to a prospective boss, I answered her apology with, "Messy desk; busy mind." It was the rationalization I always used to justify my own messes in life, both physical and metaphorical.

If my desk, bedroom, or kitchen, or life was messy it meant that I was too busy living my life to have time for cleaning it. I didn't grasp that what I really needed was a remedial course in learning how to put my toys away.

And of course, I couldn't blame my mother for it. She had already saved all those *Trudy* comics.

I am truly embarrassed to say that my organizational life was saved one day by a junk fax.

Whoever sent the fax received no benefit because I never purchased their product.

However, the cleverly "handwritten" notes in the margins of the phony magazine article fooled me into thinking it was from someone I knew.

I started searching the Internet for something that would help me with my nightmarishly messy desk.

For years people talked about how computers would one day render our lives paperless—no more newspapers (happening now), no more books (perhaps with the *Kindle, iPad,* etc.), no more messy desks (yeah right)—no more paper money.

Well, the death of paper, to paraphrase, has been greatly exaggerated.

My accountant says that he no longer stores paper copies of tax forms for posterity—only images backed up on multiple servers. However, we still kill a bunch of trees every year communicating over how I'm going to e-file my income tax return.

So, how can we deal with the avalanche of paper that continues unabated day in and day out, year after year?

Well, the solution for me came in the form of a concept embodied in a software package.

They promised that I wouldn't have to scan any documents into my computer. (Have you ever tried to scan documents reliably? Ugh!)

It was a concept so radical, so counterintuitive to how I thought about filing, that I had to watch their video tutorial three times before I implemented it for my business.

I don't mind plugging their software because I honestly feel as though they saved my life and my time and my business in so many ways.

You can find the software at www.ThePaperTiger.com. There are other programs that can accomplish the same fundamental tasks, but *The Paper Tiger* is the easiest to use, and Barbara Hemphill is fabulous.

The real genius in *The Paper Tiger* lies in its two central principles.

The first is that in order to control your paper, you have to control the flow of the paper, or more specifically, the information on the paper.

The second principle is that the flow of paper is interrupted by individuals who postpone decisions about what to do with the information on the paper.

Barbara's videos (now online) encouraged me to see the papers and other stuff on my desk as postponed decisions.

I was afraid to move anything off my desk because it was important and I was afraid that if I filed it, I would either lose it or forget about it.

I was afraid that filing the paper away would cost me money. *The Paper Tiger* also has a means for both dating and prioritizing when you need to act on your paper or the information on it.

You can put your papers away, creating a clean workspace in which you can think and work, and know that you will be able to find your papers again when you need them.

Once you become familiar and even comfortable with the process suggested by *The Paper Tiger*, there's no need to stop with your paper files.

We used to have all kinds of stuff in our basement, completely unorganized and we could never find any of it. Not anymore. We were able to organize the entire basement using our existing shelves and found many unused items that we either donated or threw away.

The same principle can also be applied to e-mails.

You need to save new contact information in the address book on your computer. You need to save some attached files in appropriate subdirectories, but most other e-mails can simply be deleted.

For a long time, I struggled with what to do with magazine and newspaper articles that I thought were worth saving.

I had the vague sense that I would like to read the articles some day and I didn't want to lose the information.

One day, however, I was reading the book *Clutter Control* and the author made two important points about these articles.

First, many magazine and newspaper articles take the form of repeated advice. You will see these articles again either in the same magazine or others like it.

Second, if you don't read it now, are you ever going to read that article?

The first point is unassailable. Magazines sell ads and they sprinkle them with content that gets rotated through seasonally or cyclically.

But if I don't want to read it now, does that mean I wouldn't read it if I were stuck in an airport, or a doctor's waiting room, or even on a bus?

Well, thanks to the Internet and cloud computing, we still don't need to save the paper clutter.

Now we can save bookmarks to these articles online, or post them to our own blog so that we can read them anytime we have Web access.

Understanding that you postpone decision-making is a huge benefit, but if you don't know why you postpone decisions, tools like *The Paper Tiger* can only solve part of the problem.

Fix the ***why*** part of your procrastinating, and tools like *The Paper Tiger* are amazingly powerful.

Chapter 12

Focus on truth

If you are lying to yourself or your customer or your family or your friends, then you won't succeed.

Unless you have a photographic memory and perfect audio recall, lies (and having to keep track of them all) will drive you crazy.

It's the meaning of the expression, "What a tangled web we weave, when first we practice to deceive." A lie will get you in trouble--even if it lets you off of some discomforting hook at first.

The "tangled web" expression gives us a primary incentive to focus on truth.

Lies cloud the mind and prevent us from thinking about productive activities, like selling more.

When my mother was five years old, my great grandfather observed that she had her, "Think tank goin' all the time."

Your think tank, your mind, is your greatest

asset. It can solve many problems.

However, if you're trying to remember what lie you told to whom and when, your think tank will come to a grinding halt.

And lies aren't the only things that can clog up your think tank.

Instead of listening to sports talk radio, or the latest kerfuffle in the news, or even which celebrity is getting divorced today, allow your think tank to get going all the time.

Give yourself quiet time every day so that your think tank has time to work. Some people call this quiet time meditation, while others call it prayer. Thomas Edison took naps. The mind is an incredible tool, but only when we give it what it needs to get the job done.

Now that you recognize that lying creates more problems than it solves, what can you do about it?

Focus on truth!

As I discussed earlier, you can discover the truth by asking yourself questions.

What do you know to be true?

Do you have defined goals you've written down?

Are you aware of your strengths?

Do you know your weaknesses?

Do you have any idea what you don't know?

How much money do you need to live on?

When you focus on the truth, it shall set you free!

Now, are there times, places, or subjects you find yourself lying about more often than others?

If there are, you should look there more closely. Use your brain's histogram or counter to help you identify where you need to focus your attention.

Ask yourself questions about why you are not focused on truth at these times. Be honest with yourself as you do.

How can we help our brain's histogram to do its job more effectively?

Keep a pad of paper or a recording device handy.

When I was in high school, the school had a great idea for dealing with the winter blahs and the post-holiday hangover. Early in January, they would sponsor an all-school "personal day"—usually on a Friday.

Well, it wasn't a real personal day and we weren't allowed to dress down in those days either.

The school administration called this all-school personal day a "Day of Concern".

This allowed the school to lecture us about drugs and alcohol one year, teen-sex another year, drugs again the following year (some kids never learn).

During my senior year, they decided to have a day devoted to The Arts—performing, studio, whatever.

As a work/study kid, my assignment was to help out a visiting painter. I was the extra pair of hands he needed to setup his easels for his live demonstrations on this "Day of Concern". While I helped him set up, he gave me a preview of how he demonstrated his favorite techniques.

I stood in open-mouthed awe, as he started in on a blank piece of canvas.

He began by putting a thick layer of charcoal over the entire surface of the canvas. Then he explained to me that the most important elements of any painting are vision and light.

You need vision to know and see what your subject will be.

You need to understand the light, and how it reflects off of the subject.

When he finally had the vision firmly placed in his mind, he gently went about rubbing the surface of the charcoal with some kind of solvent. Gradually, by removing a little bit of the charcoal layer here and there, light emerged from the darkness.

Suddenly, I could see the face that he saw so clearly in his own mind. It was the face of an elderly man that the artist had seen some time ago in Genoa, Italy.

"But how did you remember what he looked like?" I asked.

"Well," said the artist, "wherever I go, I always carry a small sketchpad in case I see something that I want to paint later. That way I won't forget the image in my head."

Since that day, I always have paper and pencil handy, or more recently my phone, to record notes for thoughts about current sales, a new book, or anything else.

You'll find that in the process of freeing up your mind, being able to focus it on what you do, thoughts will occur to you out of the blue.

Napoleon Hill referred to this kind of insight as coming from "Infinite Intelligence".

Whether it's this kind of flash of insight or a question you've worked on for weeks, you are able to remember all aspects of your thoughts later when you have more time to act on them.

In fact, I wrote most of the ideas for this book, and even much of the text, on notepads, Post-it® notes (still one of the most brilliant ideas ever), random pieces of paper from my wallet, and even napkins.

At times, I used the voice memo "App" on the *iPhone*, and this can be a useful writing tool.

My other favorite writing tool these days is the dictation software I'm using right now that's licensed from Dragon *NaturallySpeaking* by MacSpeech *Dictate*. You can talk right into your text with minimal corrections.

They even have their own "App" now.

But there are other forms and reasons for taking notes.

One of the best reasons to take notes is one I learned from computer software programmers.

You would think that guys who stare at computer screens all day wouldn't know the first thing about taking notes.

The productive ones do.

While software geeks were the first to use on-screen text editors, they have long sought ways to document their past bugs and solutions so that they don't have to waste time reinventing the wheel—again. Or worse still, repeating the same mistake they made last year when they were programming in a seldom-used computer language.

As a result, the programmers had to be really fastidious about noting and recording and then re-checking approaches to solutions that worked—and the ones that didn't.

It helps that many of them have precisely the right personality to care about accurately recording these solutions.

We can take this same process and apply it to improving our daily lives.

When you find yourself succeeding at something, try to figure out why it worked. Sit down and write about the success, analyzing the crucial decisions you made.

Likewise, when things aren't going well, start writing about why you think success isn't happening.

Writing out your thoughts is a powerful tool. You remember them more easily. And the process of working through them on paper focuses the mind in a way that thinking without writing doesn't always capture.

Recording your thoughts, especially on paper, will help you integrate your life... quickly.

Chapter 13

Accentuate the positive

I spent my early childhood years on the campuses of three different boarding schools in New England.

My father was a teacher of English literature and he coached football.

One year, he was asked to give a speech at an awards banquet.

He drew his theme for the speech from the well-known WWII song by Johnny Mercer (also sung by Bing Crosby and The Andrews Sisters): "Accentuate the positive".

I think it's important to remember that World War II came on the heels of the Great Depression, which was a time of spiritual revival in the United States.

It's how people survived.

President Roosevelt (FDR) gave a famous speech during the Great Depression that included the famous phrase, "The only thing we have to fear is...fear itself."

After the turn of our 21st century, I learned that Napoleon Hill had helped write FDR's speech. Suddenly, I became conscious of the depreciation of cultural knowledge that had affected my education in the 1970s and 1980s.

The newfound prosperity of the 1950s and early 1960s led to a loss of spirituality.

Instead of hopes and dreams for a better today and a brighter tomorrow, the news media and most of my education seemed cynically focused on how lousy everything was.

The baby-booming 1960s protesters railed against the establishment and tore down the barriers to freedom and justice for all. At the same time, they also tore down the surefootedness of most of its cultural institutions through the 1970s.

Instead of focusing on the positive aspects of our lives and our culture, we were told that we needed to wallow in the negativity as we worked through it.

Nobody bothered to read Napoleon Hill anymore.

No one listened to Dr. Maxwell Maltz.

Mainline church attendance plummeted and drug use exploded.

Fortunately, the 1960s protests have acted like a cultural Ockam's razor. When you prune a tree, you realize that the truly necessary parts are the trunk and the roots.

If you can cut away the diseased parts without killing the tree, then what you are left with can grow the following spring with renewed hope.

In the same way that a spiritual revival carried much of America through the Great Depression and WWII, we are poised now for a new spiritual resurgence. At the same time, we can choose what technological innovations suit us.

So-called atheists abound and publish profusely. At the same time, ministers like Rick Warren can interview presidential candidates.

Political correctness pervades the universities. And technology allows us to connect with support groups of every stripe and flavor.

We can say "No" to cable TV, while saying "Yes" to voicemail.

No *Xbox 360*, Yes *Wii*.

Yes on cell phone to call 911, No on texting while driving.

As long as we stay focused on the positive aspects of the things that help us, and eliminate the negativity of that which holds us back, we will succeed.

Instead of whining about whatever is bugging us in the moment, we can be grateful for how wonderful our lives really are.

Gratitude works wonders.

It's inherently positive.

The half-empty glass will always be half-full, unless we drink the contents.

If we don't like the taste of the liquid in our own glass, we can offer it to someone else to drink, trade glasses, or pour the rest down the drain.

With our newfound outlook on how much of our life we can be grateful for, we are then free to be productive rather than wallowing in self-pity and resentment.

We can choose to earn what we deserve.

The distinction between earning and deserving bugged me for a long time. I used to be frustrated trying to draw moral, political, or even existential views from these two seemingly simple words.

For example, my son was awarded the honor of being the Lead Student of the week at his school of about

250 children. One school staff member congratulated me for my son's award remarking, "I can't think of a more deserving student."

Well, did my son deserve to be Lead Student for the week because of his helpful disposition and pleasant demeanor to teachers and friends?

Or, did he earn the award by going out of his way to be helpful to teachers and by displaying consistent encouragement to his friends?

When you close a sale, do you earn your commission because you successfully followed through with your prospect from introduction to signing?

Or, did you deserve to get paid your commission because of all the hard work you put into closing the deal?

Is it an action we take that produces our outcomes—good and bad—or is it because of who we all are that we are rewarded one way versus another?

In point of fact, it's both. We earn success through preparation and hard work and we deserve success because we are willing to put in the work to begin with.

And I'm positive that it's amazing grace that brings the two together.

Chapter 14

What's your attitude about tithing?

Opinions on tithing vary widely.

Historically, tithing meant giving 10% of your income to your church.

10% was meant to pay for the church's expenses—clergy, education, worship space, and the charitable works historically associated with spiritual devotion.

Although it has roots in the laws of Moses, tithing in the Catholic Church began in the 6th century AD and has been revived over the years. Tithing was criticized under the Reformation and largely dropped by most Protestants until relatively recently.

My Granddaddy was an advocate of tithing.

When the government (at all levels) began to take over more power from the church establishment, the state also cranked up its taxation rate.

One of my favorite anti-tax songs has a refrain that goes, "If 10% is good enough for Jesus, well it ought to be enough for Uncle Sam!"

If only!

Well, since the government has an average tax rate that's higher than it used to be before there was an income tax, tithing has had to adjust.

The government now uses tax dollars to pay for charity work that the church used to perform in an *ad hoc* way, and still does. This interaction between charities of the church and the government is recognized by the tax-free status of churches.

In 2005, when Hurricane Katrina hit the Gulf Coast, many people criticized the federal government for FEMA's feeble response. However, those who were able to walk out of New Orleans north and west to safety stopped off in the churches along the interstate highway for help.

These churches took donations of mattresses (and money to buy mattresses) so that the people in need would have a decent place to sleep on the floor.

No one told the churches to do this.

Neither state nor federal nor local governments established programs for the churches to do this.

The people in the churches responded because it was the right thing to do.

So why should you tithe, and how much should you tithe?

Well, for starters, tithing is good business— people notice—and added advertising doesn't hurt.

Second, if you take your tithe seriously, you'll figure out what you care about. You don't have to give your tithe to a church, or other religious establishment. You can pick any charity, cause, or recipient as long as you've checked it out enough to know that the money isn't wasted or embezzled.

Third, you will receive insight into others and yourself that you didn't expect.

As for how much, you should shoot for 10% of what you take home.

That's my opinion.

Using take-home pay will reduce your resentment of the taxman.

In addition, tithing will help you at household budget time because you won't have to do the math twice.

Others advocate 10% of your gross.

Successful people often refer to their donations as "giving back". They want to help out the community in which they live and derive their living. Sometimes "giving back" feels like it's used more in a karmic sense when successful people talk about not losing touch with where they came from.

These successful people don't want to forget the other people who helped them along their way to success.

Another great reason to tithe is that it will change your attitude about money.

If I ask you to think about money, what thoughts pop into your head?

Take some time now to consider your attitudes about money.

Do you have enough money?

Can you afford all of the things you want?

Do you have needs that your finances don't allow?

For most of my life, I didn't know what my attitudes about money were.

I had grown up hearing phrases like, "Money is the root of all evil," and "It's not polite to talk about money," and "There's no such thing as enough money."

These three phrases reflect very different attitudes about money.

The first phrase comes from the Christian tradition and is often quoted along with an expression attributed to Jesus: "It is harder for a rich man to get into heaven than it is for a camel to fit through the eye of a needle."

Although the expression is poorly translated, its implication remains: getting into heaven is difficult when you're rich.

These ideas often suggest that eternal salvation and earthly riches are incompatible, but no one thinks to ask why.

Part of the reason for the Reformation of the Catholic Church was the notion that rich people could buy "indulgences" from the church for a price.

The concept that anyone could continue sinning guilt-free after buying forgiveness from God was anathema to most Protestants. That being said, the Church does rely on tithing from parishioners.

Without money, no church can continue to exist in the 21st century.

As for the second phrase, if it's not polite to talk about money, how do we raise the topic in the context of a sale without offending our customer?

Of course we have to talk about money. At some point we need to know how much something costs so that we can make a decision.

You can save a whole lot of time and effort if you properly qualify a customer based on price.

Price doesn't have to be the first thing you talk about with your customer. In Chapter 2, I gave you some of the questions you can ask to "break the ice" with new prospects.

I agree with the third phrase that there is no such thing as enough money. The government proves this every day.

If you carefully apply the principles in Chapter 10 on budgeting, however, you will learn how to live with "enough" money for today, so that you can make good choices rationally.

We all have to live with these conflicting and competing sayings about money that have been plucked out of context over the years. I have made some of the more difficult ones easier to understand by putting them back into context.

One of my favorite aphorisms about money is one that I drew out from the concept of money in economic theory.

Money is energy.

Allow me to explain.

We know some things are energy.

$$E = mc^2$$

A famous scientist introduced this equation last century.

He showed how energy can be produced cheaply, and how quickly our civilization could be destroyed. It explains concisely and clearly the proportions by which matter can be transformed into energy and vice versa.

With Einstein's help the U.S. figured out how to take some very heavy metals and free up their electrons to produce heat and explosive force in quantities that no one else had imagined possible.

The equation suggests that energy is simply another form of matter, however, it doesn't specify which form the energy or matter has to take.

I was never a **huge** *Star Trek* fan, but I would always marvel at how the *transporter* engineers could use the $E=mc^2$ concept to get people from starship to planet in seconds. Using the same basic idea of matter-energy transformation, the *replicator* on *The Next Generation* could make anything a *Star Fleet* officer could ever want.

The imagination of the shows' writers and producers was simply fantastic.

Imagine how straightforward life could be if we could transform energy into whatever form of matter we might like.

Well, even before Einstein and *Star Trek*, human beings sought to develop ways of turning matter into energy.

The easiest way to accomplish this goal is for everyone to agree about what constitutes energy.

Little kids do it every day at lunch.

"I'll trade you my *Ding Dong* for a *Twinkie*," or "I'll trade you a bunch of grapes for an apple."

They understand that food calories are energy.

Farmers can barter crops or they can have a barn-raising party like the Amish do. Work is energy.

It didn't take too long for people to figure out that if they could all find something that everyone valued, they could use it as money.

If they could carry it with them, then that money could act just like a battery does for electric energy.

Money is portable energy that can be transformed at the point of purchase into just about any kind of material you could need or want.

The only inventions more revolutionary than money were the light bulb (with or without a battery), and the future invention of a *Star Trek*-style *replicator*. The light bulb is still the universal icon for an idea. When someone invents the replicator one day, we will almost eliminate limits on energy use.

When that day comes, we will still need to budget our time, and we have all heard the saying, "Time is money."

Understand that if you have conflicting and negative thoughts about money, this negative energy will make it challenging for you to succeed in sales.

Money is energy that can be used for good or ill.

If you provide services or products that people need in return for money, then you have no reason at all to feel guilt for receiving money.

When you are no longer conflicted about what money is, nor resentful of others for having more than you do, then you are ready to have money flow through to you like electricity flows through to a light bulb.

Be ready to shine!

Chapter 15

Integrate your life in Twelve Steps

Be who you are everywhere and at all times.

This is what an integrated life really means.

One of the girls I knew in college was dating this brainiac at MIT whom I'll call Fred. She was completely enthralled with his brain, if not his social skills.

One day I was whining to her about how dull my advanced course on proving calculus theory was.

"I don't want an engineering degree," I whined, "but some kind of real world application of an integral once a week wouldn't hurt."

"Fred forgot how to integrate," she said quietly.

"What?"

"Fred forgot how to integrate during an exam last week," she said matter-of-factly, but with a slight giggle.

"He hasn't taken a calculus course since early in high school, and he just forgot."

Fred had my sympathy.

He was taking an exam for some upper-level math course and in the middle of the exam some professor decided to stick in some calculus as part of solving some other problem. He simply forgot how to integrate at that moment.

It's easy to forget how to live an integrated life.

Some people seem to keep it together naturally.

Others disintegrate at the slightest hiccup.

As individuals, we get so caught up in everything going on around us, that we forget how to integrate our lives.

We need to be who we are to live in peace.

So, how are we supposed to live who we are every day in a life that often feels disintegrated and disconnected?

What do you do when sales are slumping, or take a nosedive during a recession?

What do you do when everything around you looks like failure?

Well, you won't find this chapter in other books about sales.

The standard approach to dealing with a lack of successful sales or a decline in revenues is to hold the equivalent of a high school football rally...on a Monday morning. It's just how you wanted to spend your Monday morning isn't it?

The worst of these "meetings" are the ones where you go over last week's numbers, and you have to face the horrible numbers that you were dreading all weekend.

You knew what the numbers looked like on Friday and two days of worrying about them (when you should have been relaxing and recreating instead) didn't change them.

The Monday morning rallies are great, aren't they?

You get pumped up to go out and cold call people who have either never heard of your company's product or service, don't want your company's product or service, or better still, you're interrupting these people while they're trying to get their own jobs done.

Sigh.

Meanwhile actual prospects who need your product or service have no idea that you exist, let alone how to connect with you.

Does this sound very manageable?

Some people are fortunate. Whether by birth or through upbringing, they live their lives in the manner of the twelve-step programs.

They don't have to consciously think about what's happening around them, and how they're reacting to what's happening.

If they succeed in any area, they are enthused by their success. They truly enjoy their moment of victory, and then move forward to work on their next success.

If they fail, they can objectively identify the reasons for failure, formulate a solution for the problem, and then implement the solution until they achieve success.

When I started attending twelve-step meetings, I came to accept that I didn't have a successful response to failure or adversity without conscious effort. Parts of my life seemed fully functional and I felt capable, but in other areas I desperately sought any kind of control.

To illustrate how twelve-step meetings have helped me, I want to use a great analogy from one of my favorite radio talk show hosts.

I've known Ron Morris, The American Entrepreneur, for some years now, even before I was a guest on his radio show. He recently expanded his show on WMNY 1360AM in Pittsburgh into a daily drive time format.

He loves his hometown with the heart and soul of a serial entrepreneur. One of his favorite analogies is that the customers of a business can act like barnacles on a ship.

When you first start your business, you can turn on a dime and follow any promising new venture or twist in your development. Once you have some customers requiring more of your services and time, however, they can act like the buildup of barnacles on the hull of a ship.

A new clean hull glides easily through the water, but barnacles will add drag to a ship and make it slower and more difficult to maneuver. For entrepreneurs, this is often the time to sell the business to a manager or corporate structure that is better equipped to deal with the change of pace.

I look at twelve-step programs as a way to clean the barnacles off of the hull of your life's ship. As you move through your life, your mind will acquire barnacles in the form of beliefs or thought patterns and perhaps guilt, fear, or resentment that limit your think tank's natural ability to work for you.

By working a twelve-step program, you can remove these barnacle-like obstacles and sail cleanly through life's waters even if a big storm comes up.

There is a twelve-step group for almost every unwanted coping behavior that you can imagine. Alcohol, gambling, narcotics, overeating, and nicotine are the most common addictions.

Attend one of the twelve-step meetings for whatever compulsive behavior keeps you from succeeding in sales.

Give it a try.

Find out what you're missing.

Ask someone at a meeting what 30 in 30 means, or better still 90 in 90.

If you do, you'll find success beyond your wildest dreams.

If twelve steps seem too intimidating, try taking your first step in one of the programs I discussed in Chapter 10.

Remember, it's your choice.

You can live an integrated life.

Chapter 16

Do your best, and then hire a caddy

On the PGA Tour, you have professional golfers and you have professional caddies. The golfer takes the swings and the caddy holds the bag.

At least that's what it looks like from the outside.

If you ask any professional golfer in the world if he'd rather drive around the golf course in a cart and play without a caddy, he wouldn't even blink before responding:

"No!"

Why is that?

Well, caddies do more than just carry and hold the bag.

Caddies keep the clubs and balls clean for the golfer, rake bunkers and sand traps when needed. They replace divots, tend flagsticks, read greens, and obtain yardages for better club selection.

There's a lot to do during a round of golf.

Could the golfers handle it by themselves, perhaps with a handcart rather than a motorized golf cart?

Sure they could, but they happily pay at least $1,000 a week in expenses plus as much as 10% in winnings to a caddy.

Most of this work seems pretty menial, so why do caddies get paid so much?

Professional golfers pay caddies because it frees them up to do what they do best which is to swing a golf club.

Everything else is centered on that ability.

Well, in this chapter I explain why you need a caddy too.

If you play golf, you might ask, "Who can afford to have one these days? No one caddies anymore except in the pros."

If you don't play golf, then your reaction will be, "I don't even play golf, why do I need a caddy?"

Well, if you played golf, you'd enjoy it more if you played with a caddy.

However, what you really need is a caddy for your life's work.

The challenges we face in sports are often similar to challenges we face in life—and in sales.

Unless you play professionally, the nice thing about sports is that it can be practice for real-life with little or no money attached.

Few weekend golfers play with caddies anymore thanks to the ubiquity of golf carts.

Something similar has happened in the business world.

With the advent of personal computers, word-processing software, Internet access, and smart phones, the old-fashioned pairing of the secretary with the executive has gone by the wayside except at the highest executive levels.

Yes, there are receptionists, teams of secretaries that are often shared, plus paralegals and research assistants. This is fine and appeals to our sense about what constitutes productivity in the broad service sector of the economy.

And none of them comes close to having a caddy—a personal assistant.

Let's go back to the sports metaphor.

Why are caddies so important to golfers?

Because a caddy is another set of eyes and ears with a brain attached—that also happens to carry a set of clubs.

While the explosion of applied technology has helped boost productivity at minimal cost, nothing can replace a personal assistant. Having an additional brain behind your technology and business tools can dramatically propel your productivity to new heights.

Therefore, as soon as you can, as early as you can find one, and the very second you can possibly afford to, hire for yourself a personal assistant.

You're looking for honesty, competence, trustworthiness, and loyalty in that order.

With an assistant, you now have a team with a joint responsibility, rather than just you as an individual. If you can't finish a particular task, delegate it so that the rest of the project doesn't hang in limbo until you can.

It's the same principle behind the tradesman having an apprentice.

The tradesman, whether he's an electrician or a plumber, benefits from having a second pair of hands (and another brain) on the job. The apprentice learns how to work at the same time that he learns the trade.

During an internship in college, I met a financial services salesman. This guy took me everywhere he went for two days.

He had three full-time assistants working for him.

He explained to me how he trained his assistants to think like he did. Each of the assistants could ask him questions at any time all day, and the assistants handled all the work.

This salesman met with people, read, and chain-smoked all day long. He had the most productive and focused department in the entire brokerage firm.

When President Reagan and Congress reformed the U.S. income tax structure to eliminate tax deductions, this salesman turned on a dime from being the tax shelter expert to being the mutual fund guru when that market was ready to explode in volume.

He could only do that because he had assistants to handle the workload, while he stayed on the forefront of retooling his human capital knowledge base. He was in sales--not in paperwork.

Now, do you need to hire an assistant for everything?

No.

There will be times when you cannot afford an assistant.

There will be other times when outsourcing from your company or your team makes the most sense.

You don't need to spend all day deciding either.

You will find that you do many things better and quicker than your assistant can—just like the professional golfers swing their clubs better than their caddies do. You will also find that there are some things your assistant does better than you do, just like a caddy may read a particular green better than the golfer does.

If you focus on what generates the most revenue or successful sales, and let your assistant deal with the rest, then your team will be most effective.

This concept is called comparative advantage and economists have known about it since the 19th century.

It's high time to make it work for you.

Chapter 17

Sales Manager vs. Sales Mentor

A good sales manager has two primary responsibilities.

Her first responsibility is to provide guidance to each sales team member when they need help closing a successful sale.

Her second responsibility is to keep the sales team members on track toward meeting their individual, as well as team, revenue goals.

A great sales manager will also find the time and energy to be a sales mentor to her team members. While it helps to be great at selling, the sales manager does not necessarily have to be the top seller of a team.

Much of her time needs to be spent making sure that the team is prepared, and executing well.

When you finish a sales call, does your sales manager ask you questions like these?

Did you qualify the buyer properly?

Did you ask enough questions to learn what the customer needs?

Can you serve this customer's needs?

Could you have closed the deal more quickly?

If you didn't close, what else could you have done to close, or spend less time with this customer?

Ideally, a sales mentor can function like a coach in sports, or any kind of performance-based profession.

I remember the first time I saw James Earl Jones talk about how instrumental his voice coach is to his success. I thought, "Wow! *Darth Vader* needs a voice coach?"

Peyton Manning is considered to be a premier quarterback in the NFL. This is what one of his quarterback coaches said of their relationship:

> "At this level, with players like Peyton
> — who mentally is in a class by himself
> — you don't have to make it seem like
> you know more than he does, because
> you don't. But that doesn't mean I can't
> still help him. My job is not to be
> smarter than him. My job is to help him
> prepare for football games."

James Earl Jones and Peyton Manning both excel in their professions.

And they enjoy their success thanks in part to coaching and the hard work of preparation and practice.

Think carefully about the following questions:

What do you need from a sales mentor?

What do you need a sales mentor to do for you, so that you can succeed in sales?

What are the qualities you would like a sales mentor to have?

Is your current sales manager effective as a mentor?

Or do you need to look elsewhere for guidance?

Where can you find other mentors?

One of the most valuable lessons I learned in a twelve-step program is that I can choose different mentors for different areas of my life.

I find positive attributes in different people and ask them how they got where they are.

Napoleon Hill had a slightly different take on the concept of finding mentors.

He called it a Mastermind.

If you don't have personal access to the best minds in the world as mentors, you can still imagine that you do. Napoleon Hill imagined that he had a group of personal advisers, many drawn from the most intelligent historical figures like Albert Einstein, Andrew Carnegie, Julius Caesar, or Abraham Lincoln. He would then imagine what each of these historical figures would advise him about any particular question he had.

Take Napoleon Hill's advice, or seek out real mentors for your life. Remember that you don't have to go it alone.

And there's one way to find out if the individuals whom you respect are willing to mentor you.

Ask them.

Chapter 18

Horse Water Drink

I've never studied the Chinese languages, but my understanding is that there is no grammatical structure like we have in English or other Western languages.

It's a series of juxtaposed characters that are suggestive of pictures or ideas.

I have a translation of Sun Tzu's *The Art of War* with the corresponding Chinese characters alongside. It prompted me to reconsider some of the clichés we use to comment on our daily lives.

One of my favorite expressions in English is, "You can lead a horse to water, but you can't make him drink."

The other day a friend of mine was whining about a coworker who continued to ignore her advice regarding the coworker's boyfriend.

My only comment was, "Horse Water Drink".

That was my Chinese-style way to say to her, "Look, you've told her a bunch of times what to do, she's just not emotionally ready to do it yet—if she ever will be."

I learned only recently that the Italian expression translated into English for this idea is, "You can lead a donkey to the fountain, but you can't make him drink."

I think there is a connotation of stubbornness on the part of the donkey in the Italian version.

You've received a lot of useful information in this book, some of it eye opening, most of it life changing.

Are you going to take this information and act on it, using it to succeed in sales?

Or will you be the stubborn donkey in front of a gorgeous fountain, too proud or scared of the water to dip your nose in to take a drink?"

If you want to learn more about making this choice, come to my website at:

www.GeorgeWChilds.com

The choice is yours.

Choose wisely--again!

Additional copies of **_Successful Sales Without Selling Your Soul_** may be purchased from the author in bulk at a significant discount.

Email us at George@GeorgeWChilds.com to inquire—or send a FAX to 412 945-6031.